LIBERAL LEARNING AND THE ARTS OF CONNECTION FOR THE NEW ACADEMY

Elizabeth K. Minnich,
Scribe for the American Commitments National Panel

A REPORT PREPARED FOR
AMERICAN COMMITMENTS

A NATIONAL INITIATIVE OF THE
ASSOCIATION OF AMERICAN COLLEGES
AND UNIVERSITIES

THIS WORK WAS SUPPORTED BY A GRANT FROM THE
FORD FOUNDATION

Published by
Association of American Colleges and Universities
1818 R Street, NW
Washington, DC 20009

Copyright 1995

ISBN 0-911696-66-0
Library of Congress Catalog Card No. 95-80685

TABLE OF CONTENTS

THE AMERICAN COMMITMENTS NATIONAL PANEL

Suzanne Benally
Project Director,
The Institute on Ethnic Diversity,
Western Interstate Commission
for Higher Education

Alfred H. Bloom
President,
Swarthmore College

Johnnella Butler
Professor of American
Ethnic Studies,
University of Washington

Carlos Cortés
Professor of History,
University of California–Riverside

Bonnie Thornton Dill
Professor of Women's Studies,
University of Maryland

Troy Duster
Professor of Sociology,
University of California–Berkeley

Ramón Gutiérrez
Chair, Ethnic Studies Department,
University of California–
San Diego

Patrick J. Hill
Professor of Interdisciplinary
Study,
Evergreen State College

Harry H. Kitano
Professor of Social Welfare
and Sociology,
University of California–
Los Angeles

Lee Knefelkamp
Professor of Higher and Adult
Education,
Teachers College,
Columbia University

Elizabeth K. Minnich
Professor of Philosophy,
The Union Institute

Caryn McTighe Musil
Senior Research Associate,
Association of American Colleges
and Universities

Gayle Pemberton
Professor of African American
Studies,
Wesleyan University

Carol Schneider, ex officio
Executive Vice President,
AAC&U,
Director, American Commitments
Initiative

Uri Treisman
Professor of Mathematics,
University of Texas–Austin

Frank Wong
Provost and Vice President
for Academic Affairs,
University of Redlands
*Frank Wong served as chair of the
National Panel until his untimely
death in April 1995.*

FOREWORD

This report from AAC&U's American Commitments initiative explores the connections among diversity, democratic aspirations, and goals for student learning in higher education. Drawing on new fields and emphases in contemporary scholarship, it points higher education toward the learning we need in a world of extraordinary heterogeneity and profound inequalities.

Around the country, those who see integral connections between the future of higher education and the future of our society have been calling on the academy to reinvent itself. The promising message of this report is that the renewal we need is already under way. An old era is coming to a close; a new vision of the intimate connections between higher learning and the quality of human community is coming clearly into focus.

The academy has always placed education for civic responsibility at the core of its educational mission. *Liberal Learning and the Arts of Connection for the New Academy* challenges us to think in fresh terms about the meaning of that commitment. What kind of learning helps prepare students to assume responsibility and leadership in a democracy characterized by diversity and marred by persistent and invidious inequalities? How do we move beyond the dichotomized thinking that frustrates contemporary efforts to describe and advance a generative pluralism? What are the connections between studying justice and creating a more just society for all participants?

Writing on behalf of the National Panel guiding AAC&U's American Commitments initiative, scribe Elizabeth Minnich observes that a "new academy" is growing up around the edges—and increasingly within the departments—of the "old" academy. This new academy explores and gives voice to communities that traditionally have had no role or marginalized roles on our campuses. It welcomes rather than avoids critical and creative engagement with wider communities. It endorses and produces scholarship that seeks not just to know the world but to work toward a better world.

Scholars and teachers in this emergent "new academy" are pioneering ways of thinking, learning, and teaching that provide models for engaging differences constructively, rather than divisively. In their work, "diversity" is not simply new subject matter, although the new academy has contributed in stunning ways to the expansion and reconfiguration of knowledge. Diversity calls for new capacities, new ways of thinking and acting and relating. This report describes those capacities and the kinds of learning that develop them. It encourages us to move beyond the so-called culture wars to a new era in which all of us learn better how to make a world in which everyone is heard and everyone counts.

THE AMERICAN COMMITMENTS INITIATIVE	This report is sponsored by AAC&U's national initiative, American Commitments: Diversity, Democracy, and Liberal Learning. Launched with an initial grant from the Ford Foundation in 1993, American Commitments has focused on diversity in relation to educational mission and to the nation's democratic aspirations and values. By highlighting the social nexus in which all learning occurs, the American Commitments linkage between diversity and democratic society challenges us to think more deeply about what individuals learn from their experience of campus ethos—and how that learning in turn constrains or enriches the quality and vitality of American communities.

American Commitments comprises four distinct but interrelated activities: development of policy reports and recommendations about higher education's role in a diverse democracy; institutes on American pluralism and campus leadership; a network of institutions working on general education curriculum planning and faculty development around diversity and community; and electronic, workshop, and print development of resource materials to support campus diversity efforts. Currently, more than one hundred colleges and universities are working in this initiative to recast their general education curricula and create more inclusive campus communities. Dozens of other institutions have sent campus teams to working conferences sponsored by American Commitments.

THE AMERICAN COMMITMENTS NATIONAL PANEL REPORTS	The work of the American Commitments initiative has been guided by members of the National Panel, a group of scholars, teachers, and academic administrators who have each made significant contributions to contemporary understandings of diversity in higher education and United States society. Panel members brought their own diversities—societal, experiential, intellectual—to the American Commitments dialogue, not as suppressed background but as the context for everything they know and value and work for as leaders in higher education.

Members of the Panel have held a remarkable series of dialogues, in the group as a whole, in smaller subsets of the Panel, and with higher education colleagues at a series of working conferences throughout the country. Panel members' analyses of connection and commitment in American society, deepened, complicated, and reconfigured through two years of internal and public discussions of several draft reports, culminate in the publication of the report in this volume and others in this series.

Together, these National Panel reports provide a comprehensive examination of higher education's missions of leadership and service in a society that is diverse, divided by legacies of social and gender hierarchy, and yet still embarked on a historic wager that democratic dialogue across difference can lead all participants toward achievement of a just and equitable society.

In its commitment to diversity, higher education assumes both a distinctive responsibility and a precedent-setting challenge. While other institutions in the society also seek and foster diversity, higher education is uniquely positioned, by its mission, values, and dedication to learning, to foster and nourish the habits of heart and mind that Americans need to make diversity work in daily life. We have an opportunity to help our campuses experience engagement across difference as a value and a public good.

HIGHER EDUCATION AS A TESTING GROUND FOR AMERICAN PLURALISM

Across the country, our nation's campuses have become a highly visible stage on which the most fundamental questions about difference, equality, and community are being enacted. But higher education's work is more complicated than many realize by the reality that, in the communities beyond our campus boundaries, residential segregation has been increasing, not decreasing. As we noted in the first report in this series, *The Drama of Diversity and Democracy*:

> Two-thirds of Americans now live in those combinations of cities and their surrounding suburbs that the Bureau of the Census designates as Standard Metropolitan Statistical Areas. But whether we look at the distribution of populations in these SMSAs as a whole or at the composition of the urban core within them, the striking demographic trend is the intensification, not the diminution, of racial residential segregation. Even as the nation's laws have pressed Americans toward new forms of equality and connection, Americans have not only resisted residential integration but compounded and consolidated earlier twentieth-century patterns of residential segregation.

These developments mean that colleges and universities committed to diversity as a positive educational value assume the special responsibility of fostering capacities for and commitments to pluralism that are often not part of Americans' neighborhood experience. For many students, attending a college or university may be their first extended experience of a notably heterogeneous community. Participation in an intensive community drawn from multiple cultures and histories calls on a disposition to engage and learn across difference that many students have had no opportunity to achieve. It requires skills that have not been practiced—or valued.

This report and the others in this series describe ways that higher education can respond to this fundamental challenge in the American narrative. Formed as we are by the academy's strong traditions of intellectual and social pluralism, higher education faces a rich opportunity to put its own commitments to learning at the nation's service.

CAROL SCHNEIDER
Director, The American Commitments Initiative

ACKNOWLEDGMENTS

The Association of American Colleges and Universities extends warm thanks to the Ford Foundation which provided grant support that enabled AAC&U to launch the American Commitments initiative and the work of the National Panel. We are especially grateful to Edgar Beckham, program officer in education and culture at the Ford Foundation, whose vision and commitment have helped hundreds of colleges and universities develop productive ways to educate students for the diversities and possibilities of the world they inherit. We also extend our thanks to Alison Bernstein, director of education and culture at the Ford Foundation, for her continuing confidence in AAC&U's work on equity and diversity. In addition we thank the National Endowment for the Humanities (NEH), which has also supported the American Commitments initiative.

Thanks are due as well to Paula Brownlee, president of AAC&U, for her support of this initiative and for constructive readings of the Panel reports.

AAC&U and members of the National Panel express particular gratitude for the leadership of Frank Wong, historian and, during his service on the Panel, academic vice president of the University of Redlands. Frank Wong served as chair of the National Panel until his death from cancer in April 1995. He provided a moral center for Panel discussions during his tenure and left all participants in the American Commitments initiative a lasting legacy of fidelity to justice, compassion, and the unfinished promise of United States democracy.

The analysis presented in this report was developed in a series of small group meetings involving members of the National Panel. Elizabeth Minnich served as scribe for the National Panel. All of those who took part in these dialogues thank her for her encompassing vision, moral commitment, and extraordinary intellect.

Earlier drafts of this paper were discussed with academic administrators and faculty members at an American Commitments leadership institute held at Georgetown University in September 1993, at several dozen small group sessions at the AAC&U annual meeting in Washington, D.C., in January 1994, at a national conference on cultural pluralism sponsored by the Washington Center for Undergraduate Education in January 1995, and at a Midwest Faculty Seminar cosponsored by the University of Chicago and the Association of American Colleges and Universities in April 1995.

We extend our thanks to all those who gave the Panel constructive suggestions as we worked through the complex ideas and issues addressed in these pages. They helped us see that the ideas presented in this report were both important and profoundly challenging to the daily assumptions of many faculty members and academic leaders. We have tried to respond to both these insights in this final version of the report.

All members of the Panel owe great thanks to Maureen McNulty, who as a special assistant to the Panel has contributed editorial skill, bibliographical zeal, and organizational devotion to the Panel's work. While Maureen McNulty was on maternity leave, Charlotte Hogsett ably served as editor-advisor to the project. In addition, we thank Kathleen Connelly, Kevin Hovland, Debra Humphreys, and Suzanne Hyers, all members of the American Commitments staff who have done an outstanding job in collectively organizing the institutes at which Panel reports were discussed.

Finally, we acknowledge the commitment, competence, and support of AAC&U's communications department, which prepared this report for publication. Joann Stevens, vice president for communications, helped develop the format for the reports. Cindy Olson brought creativity, skill, and wonderful patience in creating the design for a report that remained in dialogue almost to the moment of publication. Thanks also to Amy Wajda and Heather Collins for their proofreading and copyediting.

SYNOPSIS

Diversity has been cast as a problem for both democracy and liberal education. This framing tells us that prevailing conceptions of democracy, of education, and of their relations are not serving us well. What kind of democracy, what kind of education, cannot deal with given and historical differences among humankind? We believe our diversities, from the benign to the most viciously inequitable, are resources for liberal learning in a nation with aspirations to democracy. What we do not know we can neither celebrate nor face and change, either on campus or in what ought to be our common civic life.

A "new academy" has already appeared on our campuses. It comprises ways of thinking, reconfigurations of disciplines, new modes of teaching and assessment, and new forms of scholarship. All of these have developed precisely in order to move beyond historically inequitable divisions among us.

We therefore bring some of what may be learned from the new academy into conversation with prevailing traditions. Such conversation brings forward for serious discussion some of the basic issues before us today. They include:

- issues of *inclusion/exclusion* of "kinds" of people, as citizens and as learners, teachers, and subjects in liberal education;

- issues of the *relations* among individuals, communities, societies, cultures, and polities taught about and practiced in education;

- issues of the historical, social, cultural, and political *contexts* of knowledge creation and preservation; and

- issues of how we may, and why we should, search for more inclusive and equitable *common grounds*.

Drawing on the rich mine of work already available and still developing on such issues in virtually all fields, we present for discussion some shifts in concepts and ways of thinking. We focus on the reframing of thinking and related reconfigurations of liberal arts. We are looking for ways to open spaces for more relational thinking, and for more inclusive courses, teaching, scholarship, and action.

We are looking for ways to open spaces for more relational thinking, and for more inclusive courses, teaching, scholarship, and action.

We do not present the ways of thinking and shifts in meanings and practices explored here as settled, nor do we see them as panaceas. We offer them as invitations to engage in the difficult and exciting effort to evaluate and risk changing even some of our more deeply ingrained habits of thought—the very effort to which we invite our students in liberal education.

We propose, then, to open a discussion about how we can:

- be reflective about *ways of thinking* that do and do not help us move beyond old divisions, oppositions, and hierarchies;

- include the *subjects and competencies of the new academy* as they help us reconfigure the liberal arts in order to engage them more fully with the quest for an open, generative civic life;

- purposefully seek to develop the *arts of translation*, abilities, commitments, and knowledge required to move respectfully and productively among subjects and fields, individuals, communities, cultures, and nations;

- practice with our students and colleagues democratic *arts of associative living*, acting, and learning;

- make more permeable in both directions the boundaries between *town and gown;*

- teach and pursue our scholarship in such a way that we and our students become both more grounded and more able fully to *recognize* each other, so that we may welcome our mutual responsibilities to each other and the world we share; and

- through such efforts, continue to try to live up to our claim that liberal education has as one of its fundamental purposes *preparing students for lives as active citizens* in a country still aspiring to democracy within an increasingly interdependent but hardly yet equitable world.

RETHINKING THE "PROBLEM OF DIVERSITY"

Across the United States, the "problem of diversity" is the subject of many, often heated, discussions and almost as many creative projects. Many educators have taken the challenge seriously, and hope that they have been responsible in beginning, at least, to address it. But the framing of the problem is itself problematic and revealing.

- What conceptions of liberal education are challenged by the given that humans differ from each other in many ways?

- For what kind of democracy is human plurality a problem?

- What is it about liberal learning in its historically complex relations with democracy that establishes diversity as a problem rather than a resource?

Remembering history, we focus especially on how we may think together now in fresh ways about liberal education in a country that would be democratic. We engage many of the too often separate conversations on campuses, weaving them together where possible while making our own suggestions for reframing thinking and practices.

We do not present what we suggest as finished, nor as a panacea. Instead, we offer it as an invitation to engage in the effort to which all students of liberal education are called: to reflect on habits of thought and familiar frameworks in the light of new subjects, critiques, and alternatives.

What we think about, and with whom, is always important. So, too, is how we think.

For what kind of democracy is human plurality a problem?

INTRODUCTION

THE LIBERAL ARTS AND THE NEW ACADEMY

At the crux of the fierce debate [about education in this multicultural nation]…is the meaning of America: who are we, who belongs, who determines, who controls, whose values prevail, in whose image shall the country be made? Are we a civilization in decline because we cannot agree at this point on "national culture," or are we at an exciting crossroads, engaged in lively debate about our national future?
—Evelyn Hu-DeHart

Origins persist in having influence even when forms have changed dramatically. Liberal education is by no means entirely free of the exclusiveness of the centuries during which it developed. Nevertheless, there have indeed been dramatic, even transformative, changes. The arts of the trivium and quadrivium, the classical and religious studies that were once open only to a very few privileged males, bear little resemblance to the marketplace-like jumble of disciplines taught to many more students today. But it is not incorrect to call either "liberal arts." There are no essential liberal arts inscribed somewhere by a suprahuman wisdom.

Liberal learning in the United States is and has been, in fact, a particular, tangled thread within the history of higher education, itself a record, as the historian of education Frederick Rudolph (1977) notes, "of how the American people faced such matters as who were to be their leaders, whether the society was to be governed by an elite, and how far the concept of equality was to be carried in the provision of courses of study appropriate not just for the few but for the many."

In education as in the nation, and for related reasons, the one created from many has never been unitary, equally inclusive, unchallenged, or unchanging, and it is not so today. We have not lost a "common culture" or a securely unchanging "higher" culture, either. This country has always both torn and created itself through its "manyness." It is doing so again today in response to the generative tensions captured by the title of the Association of American Colleges and Universities' initiative, American Commitments: Diversity, Democracy, and Liberal Learning.

The latest intense phase of national discussions in the American tradition of reinventing education in relation to struggles over what democracy should be, and for whom, has been going on for more than thirty-five years. A "new academy" has already emerged from the ferment. It comprises ways of thinking, teaching, and creating scholarship that have developed in response to the unsound, historically inequitable divisions of humans that have both distorted and driven the American dream of equality for all. The new academy both provides an implicit and explicit critique of the old and suggests how we may move beyond what is by reconceptualizing and broadening the very idea of liberal learning.

MAPPING THE NEW ACADEMY

Imagine a campus, unlike yours, perhaps, but familiar. At the center are buildings that house administrative and professionalized disciplines' departmental offices, classrooms, spaces for lectures, plays, dances, and concerts. Many of these are ivy-covered. Near to these are the dormitories, and dotted around them are striking, sparkling new buildings that house programs well supported by the private sector. All these buildings are evidently strong. The material of which they are built as well as their design asserts their importance and bespeaks continuity from the past, a confident present, an assured future. Large doors lead into them, and often new ramps provide access up flights of stairs; many windows mark their walls; neat paths connect them with each other. Characteristically, the buildings are not well marked, so a stranger is easily lost unless she or he can find an insider not only willing but able to give good directions. Although there are parking lots and spaces, there is never enough room.

On the periphery, there are slightly shabby houses now owned by the university. These are often hard to distinguish from the community that has relinquished them, except for discreet (but carefully set out) signs in the front yard: Women's Studies, African American Studies, Center for Collaborative Learning, Swedish American Studies, Environmental Studies, American Indian Studies, Gay and Lesbian Studies, Peace Studies, Deaf Studies, Multicultural Studies, Hispanic Studies, Ethnic Studies, Labor Studies, Interdisciplinary Studies, Science and the Humanities programs, Asian American Studies, Holocaust Studies, Institute for Technology and Values, Cultural Studies, Center for Research on Teaching and Learning, Continuing Education Center. Here are the programs that began, at least, on "soft" money, in somewhat dilapidated if lovingly decorated spaces, in houses that still have kitchens. Some of them have ramps and other provisions to make them accessible, but some have not been given the money needed to make changes in old buildings. Their regular denizens feel the contradiction between that failure and their commitments acutely, and compensate in many ingenious ways so as to welcome all who come.

These houses are on the campus—but not really; in the community—

but not really. The people who work here also have offices (perhaps shared) "on campus." Having earned doctorates and positions in one of the presently prevailing departmental disciplines, they have chosen to work "the double shift" of maintaining their status in a "real" department, as well as in the "program" they helped conceive and birth which always seems to need more of their nurturing attention. The students for whom these houses frame safe spaces for community and learning help take care of them, even as they themselves ask for care. There is really no parking; the street and perhaps a driveway must suffice. The proper campus paths do not reach to these buildings. To gain them, one must cross busy streets, and those who work in these programs do so regularly.

Today, many campuses look like that, although some have very few of the newer programs, or do offer them but keep them institutionally very marginal. Others, however, have already reached across their inherited boundaries so well that they have created a tensely exciting, creative mix of people, communities, and programs that led someone to call such campuses "cauldrons of democracy." It is in these spaces that the academy is learning how to value and encompass the range of human diversities.

What is today called diversity is comprised of interrelated but distinct strands. At base, it involves the givens that each and every one of us is unique, at the same time as we are all nourished by cultures that both overlap and differ. But because human histories are marred by faulty thinking and injustices that have created vicious inequalities among these individual and cultural differences, our "common differences" too often rank and divide rather than simply distinguish us. In these "cauldrons of democracy," the new academy attempts to melt those invidious divisions, not the differences that make us all who we are. When access is not limited to the historically privileged few, democracy engages diversity. Framings of what diversity is and means begin to shift in recognition of the need to deal better than we have with the complexities of many kinds of human differences and similarities.

The new academy is to be found in the "special" programs and emerging fields variously placed on our campuses.

The new academy is to be found, then, in the "special" programs and emerging fields variously placed on our campuses. It is influencing virtually all disciplines now, as many work to comprehend the differing sources and meanings of our diversities and to undo old injustices that, built into assumptions from earlier times, still skew efforts to think well about humankind and our relations to each other and to the earth we share. But such efforts are not brand new or characteristic only of our own times. Earlier understandings of liberal education in relation to diversities differ from contemporary approaches in important ways and cannot be relied on to frame today's commitments and ways of thinking. Nevertheless, they

**THE IDEA OF A
UNIVERSITY PAST**

3

There is a shared

understanding that higher

education must face the

distortions of the past

and struggle to correct them

if it is to live up

to its present aspirations.

are part of the story of the relation of liberal education to issues of diversity. They remind us of the long-recognized, if differently conceived, mutuality of the quests for truth and for justice in and through liberal education.

In May of 1852, Cardinal John Henry Newman, rector of the new Catholic University of Ireland, began a series of inaugural discourses that became one of the most influential books on higher education written in the West, *The Idea of a University*. Newman's vision included recognition that universities are involved in humankind's quests for freedom and justice as well as knowledge. He wrote, "In the times now opening upon us, nationalities are waking into life" and "The wrongs of the oppressed…are brought under the public opinion of Europe" so that "retribution is demanded and exacted for past crimes in proportion to their heinousness and their duration." As Jaroslav Pelikan notes, in his 1992 reconsideration of Newman's work, "What was called for was a university that would help make reparations for those crimes, on behalf not only of the Irish but of all the oppressed and underdeveloped 'nationalities' and peoples of the earth."

Newman's dreamt-of solution was to provide access to education for all under the aegis of what he took to be universal principles. He wrote:

> I am turning my eyes toward a hundred years to come, and I dimly see the island I am gazing on, become the road of passage and union between two hemispheres, and the centre of the world….[I]n it I see a flourishing University….Thither, as to a sacred soil, the home of their fathers, and the fountain-head of their Christianity, students are flocking from East, West, and South, from America and Australia and India, from Egypt and Asia Minor, with the ease and rapidity of a locomotion not yet discovered, and last, though not least, from England—all speaking one tongue, all owning one faith, all eager for one large true wisdom; and thence, when their stay is over, going back again to carry over all the earth "peace to men of good will."

Newman was unusual for his belief that so many were capable of attaining the education of which he dreamed. But however eloquent, heartfelt, and well-intentioned, this is hardly a vision of unity acceptable to those who speak different tongues, follow different faiths, or would have been excluded on grounds of gender regardless. Pelikan, who not only admires but identifies himself with Newman, nevertheless realizes that he must update the framing and terms of Newman's recognition that the university plays a role in rectifying injustices of the past. Pelikan writes:

> The university must exercise a major share of leadership in redeeming the pledge of equality, by insisting that what Tocqueville called "the means of exercising mental endowments" truly become equally

available….In doing so, the university must go on striving to eliminate from its own programs of student admissions and faculty appointments as well as from its curriculum the vestiges of discrimination and prejudice against race, class, or gender that still remain.

There is here, threading across historical eras and differing political, religious, and philosophical commitments, a shared understanding that higher education must face the distortions of the past and struggle to correct them if it is to live up to its present aspirations. At the same time, there have been and are today sharply differing understandings of how we should take up this central educational political task.

To claim that all "vestiges of discrimination" must be removed from educational practices implies a kind of housecleaning whereby one sweeps obstacles away and makes the house of learning accessible to and appropriate for all. But perhaps cleaning will not be adequate. Perhaps it will be necessary, further, to add on a series of annexes intended to accommodate those for whom there was not room before. But it may well be that a more thoroughgoing renovation will be called for, one that will entail redefining the very notion of house, so that we will stop confusing one kind of house, one idea of a university, with what all must be.

The new academy, then, is informed by ideas of multiversities that already exist and are themselves being changed by the academy emerging today. The new academy shapes as it reflects our times, as ideas of a university in the past shaped and reflected theirs. Democracy, which in this country as elsewhere has often been in tension with higher education, is also being once again re-created. Liberal education must play a crucial role in this process. As the AAC&U mission statement affirms,

> Liberal learning aims to be a productive force in the life of a democratic and pluralistic society by challenging all citizens equally to master the complexities of self-governance, to see and appreciate issues from contrasting points of view, to value human and cultural diversity, to discover priorities, and to make informed choices.

The American Commitments National Panel believes that it is time to reframe what and how we think in multivocal, translational conversations among many more than have ever before been included as equals. We do not, then, choose to enter what has been too often cast as a debate between two "sides." *Instead of arguing or debating, we reconsider, drawing on diversities of many kinds for the self-knowledge and self-governance of a humankind less fearfully divided into "us" and "them."* Toward that goal, we focus here on ways liberal education can help us to think together as equals in shared public life on and off campus.

The new academy shapes as it reflects our times, as ideas of a university in the past shaped and reflected theirs.

CHAPTER ONE

RECONSIDERING TRADITIONS, RECONFIGURING KNOWLEDGE

It seems increasingly probable that Western culture is in the middle of a fundamental transformation: A "shape of life" is growing old. In retrospect, this transformation may be as radical (but as gradual) as the shift from a medieval to a modern society. Accordingly, this moment in the history of the West is pervaded by a profound yet little comprehended change, uncertainty, and ambivalence. This transitional state makes certain forms of thought possible and necessary, and it excludes others.
—Jane Flax

Discussions of what knowledge is and of what grounds we may claim for its significance, worth, and soundness are common in virtually all fields now.

The emergence of the new academy and the transitional time for liberal education it signals is in part evidenced by the striking emphasis on epistemological questions in a great deal of today's scholarship. Discussions of what knowledge is and of what grounds we may claim for its significance, worth, and soundness are common in virtually all fields now. Such self-conscious reflectiveness among scholars is heightened by pressures from outside as well as inside the academy calling on us to account for ourselves. Today, those pressures come from legislatures tightening their budgets and eyeing ours; from boards of trustees; from established cultural institutions and funders; from critics and defenders of present liberal arts offerings; from populations too long excluded or underserved; and from those who know themselves to be lessened by the injustice of unequal access to knowledge.

At this point in history, in our scholarship and in our teaching, we are called upon not just to add to or pass on a stock or store of knowledge, but to *think about what we are doing*. This process may help us undo the old hierarchical divide between thought and action, and between education and citizenship, that has made it too easy for thinkers to disclaim, and for others to deny, the relation of such work to the changing world we share.

At the same time we as scholars and teachers are rethinking our work, others are rethinking citizenship to make it, too, both coherent and comprehensive. As the Kettering Foundation's *Civic Declaration: A Call for a New Citizenship* put it,

We commit ourselves to a common citizenship that honors difference and incorporates diversity. From the myriad races, cultures, and communities of interest that are America, we draw shared values rooted not in sameness, but in the common ground of our shared tasks and obligations to future generations....Citizenship is a bond that holds potential to unite people of radically diverse backgrounds, ages, and viewpoints. It allows us to enter public life with equal dignity, no matter what our social or economic status.

In conversation with those who are redefining citizenship in this way, educators may hope to emerge from these fertile times better able to explain our work to the broader polity and the many communities we serve whose support is so crucial to us. At present, we find it hard to make that case, and it will probably continue to be so during these times of transition. But we are learning how to explain what we are about in terms that are more appropriate to today's aspirations and needs than those we have inherited from times in which only the few were to be educated not to work for a living but to live "the life of the mind." (The word "scholar" derives from the Greek for "leisure.") We will help others understand the relations between liberal learning and democratic aspirations better as we ourselves understand them better, as we reconfigure the old terms that made us diverse in inegalitarian ways, skewing constructions of knowledge and pedagogies just as they distorted practices of public, social, and economic life.

The tradition that is changing comes in various guises and combinations, as the Greco-Roman tradition, the Euro-American tradition, the tradition of the Enlightenment and of colonialism, the new world or modern versions of old world or classic heritages. In these or other framings, each of these separately and all of them together have today been subjected to energetic critiques, and equally energetic defenses, from inside and outside of higher education. Few scholars can speak today as effortlessly or unself-consciously as they did only a decade ago about the "heritage of Western Civilization." Every term in that phrase is now the site of both critique and creative scholarship emerging from disciplinary offices as well as from the "special studies" that mark most visibly the reconfiguring of liberal learning.

To some, all these changes confirm the view that a new "shape of life" is emerging that may be more authentically democratic as it is released from old errors of ignorance and prejudice, and the related unfairness of differential access to resources. Others proclaim, on the contrary, that we have slid far down a slippery slope toward intellectual and moral chaos and strife.

Such tension is not new; rather it is as characteristic of the country as

The tradition that is changing comes in various guises and combinations, as the Greco-Roman tradition, the Euro-American tradition, the tradition of the Enlightenment and of colonialism.

of its versions of liberal arts education. In the famous *Federalist No. 10*, James Madison gave voice to fears of loss of order and hence of justice in an uncontrolled democracy. "Complaints are everywhere heard," he wrote, "that the public good is disregarded in the conflicts of rival parties, and that measures are too often decided, not according to the rules of justice and the rights of the minor party, but by the superior force of an interested and overbearing majority."

That today it is "minorities" whose interests, programs, scholarship seem (oddly, in fact) "overbearing" to some in one sense does not matter: the old tensions are still with us. Admitting both our differences and inequitable diversities leads some to proclaim the death of civilization, the disuniting of America, the collapse of scholarship into rampant, subjective relativism. Others, standing in the revolutionary, egalitarian tradition that has also always been American, try to understand how today's challenges relate to those values. And some, having been denied equality, angrily and creatively challenge the very idea that there has been a united culture or an egalitarian tradition, calling on this country finally to face, so that it can transcend, its failures.

As educators involved with today's critical evaluations and reconfigurations of knowledge, this Panel is clear. We have no desire to return to the kind of unity once found in curricula of schools that excluded most of us, not on the basis of our ability, or our historical and cultural significance to humankind or to this country, but solely and cruelly and ignorantly because of preconstituted (pre-judicial) categories that marked some kinds of us as inferior, not worthy of inclusion. We believe that liberal learning in institutions no longer locked into old exclusive, hierarchical practices requires changes not only in admissions, but also in what is taught, and how. Our task is not only to add, but to transform.

Knowledge created when the old exclusions were believed by many scholars and citizens to reflect adequate—even universal—truths about humankind is obviously likely to be biased, not just incomplete. It must be carefully critiqued lest hidden as well as overt assumptions continue to distort our best efforts at less prejudiced inquiry.

Just as no one kind of person should be held to be capable and worthy of higher education, and no one kind of person should be held to be capable and worthy of full citizenship, no one tradition's universalized view of truth, beauty, goodness should be imposed on the diverse experiences, heritages, communities, values, and commitments of humankind in ways that refuse them serious consideration.

Liberal learning in institutions no longer locked into old exclusive, hierarchical practices requires changes not only in admissions, but also in what is taught, and how.

CHAPTER TWO
ARTS OF TRANSLATION

Society not only continues to exist by transmission, by communication, but it may fairly be said to exist in transmission, in communication....To be a recipient of a communication is to have an enlarged and changed experience. One shares in what another has thought and felt and insofar, meagerly or amply, has his own attitude modified. Nor is the one who communicates left unaffected....The experience has to be formulated in order to be communicated. To formulate requires getting outside of it, seeing it as another would see it, considering what points of contact it has with the life of another so that it may be got into such form that he can appreciate its meaning....Only when [communication] becomes cast in a mold and runs in a routine way does it lose its educative power.
—John Dewey

It is possible, if not simple, to find complementarities in differences.

We welcome critiques of the tradition and today's reconfigurations of knowledge in an emerging new academy for which diversities of many kinds are understood as resources for all, not the problems of some. We believe that it is possible, if never simple, intellectually as in our communities and polity to form bonds that honor distinctions and multiplicities. It is possible, if not simple, to find complementarities in differences. The situation in which we find ourselves today provides opportunities to think better than we have about our individual and cultural differences in relation to those created by unjust, untruthful human systems. It calls us to reflect anew on the multiple meanings of community, civic life, and nation in relation not only to individuals but to cultures. And it reminds us to think about how the love of truth and of justice challenges us to remain engaged with the differing worlds to which our arts of knowledge relate us. Indeed, we trust that we can, if we will, come together precisely in order to think through and act to change that which has divided us, and thus also to affirm the possibility of an open, mutually comprehensible, and valued public life.

Liberal learning does not need to provide a preordained common ground for all who would become educated. Instead, it can bring us together, as egalitarian democracy does, to practice the arts of learning, listening, speaking, questioning, interpreting, judging, choosing, acting in the freedom that pursuit of wisdom requires. Socrates, we remember, was

11

called by Plato the best citizen Athens ever had, not because of what he knew but because he spent his life in the marketplace engaging others in conversations that undid old certainties. Together with his teacher, Diotima, Socrates taught that wisdom is something we love and yearn for. It is not something any of us alone possesses.

Leadership is already present on our campuses in the shared quests for more capacious wisdom. Leadership emerges from all the spaces of discussion and connection on campuses that have been cauldrons of democracy for some time. We find knowledgeable and practiced leaders in departmental and administrative offices; student centers; the houses for "special" studies that negotiate communication between the "real" world and the "ivory tower"; student affairs offices that teach skills of mediation and communication; science and technology programs that work with differing learning styles and that challenge students to solve intellectual problems taking account of the cultural and value-freighted contexts in which they arise; and more—in classrooms that respectfully engage the differing lives and passions of those who meet together there. Such leaders are practiced not only in mediating but in translating, helping us learn to work with and across differences. These are invaluable skills in a time of consciousness of reconfiguring boundaries.

The liberal arts for today should no longer rest on preordained common ground made up, in part at least, of particular, historically limited ideas and ideals claimed to be universal that, in practice, were too often used to justify exclusions and expropriation. Nor can liberal learning renounce responsibility for what may be common in favor only of what is different.

What we need now are arts of translation that bring us together as we practice them. Informed by knowledge of the meanings between which they translate, we commit ourselves to comprehension and communication far beyond narrow expertise or sectarian partialities.

If, for now, we explore liberal education as involving quests to discern, conceptualize, and practice arts of translation, we can face divisions arising even from the worst of the old failures of justice and knowledge. Studying the histories of those who have worked to overcome such failures, we can develop a more capacious vision. James H. Cone (1993), for example, compares, contrasts, relates, distinguishes, and connects where others have felt there was no option but to choose sides. He turns even a "nightmare" into a resource for learning and a new vision:

> Without confronting the American nightmare that Malcolm bore witness to, we will never be able to create the beloved community articulated so well by Martin King....Blacks must begin with Malcolm, that is, with a healthy regard for themselves—their history and culture as it stretches back to the continent of Africa. But we

What we need now are arts of translation that bring us together as we practice them.

must not stop with Malcolm....We also must critique Malcolm and Martin for their failures, especially their blatant sexism, and their silence on homophobia in the black community....They were only human beings with assets and liabilities like all of us....Let us, therefore, create an America—not just for Martin and Malcolm, or for whites and blacks but for Hispanics, Indians, and Asians and for women in all groups, for gay men and lesbians—for every people, every culture and every faith in this land.

This, too, is a dream of commonality, one that aspires to include many people and cultures without insisting on homogenization, without demonizing some to justify excluding them, or needing to sanctify others to defend their importance. It is thus a more democratic aspirational ideal than those that, locked in past prejudices, believe any one group can set a standard for either knowledge or community.

Such an ideal asks big things of us, more than perhaps we can quite comprehend. But it also asks that we prepare for such comprehension, and the actions it elicits, by practicing arts of translation in all that we do. Translation across oppositional positions can be practiced in inquiry that not only follows disciplinary forms but also risks crossing borders; in analyses and syntheses, theories, and practices that are used to check and correct each other; in appraisals of values that are undertaken self-reflectively; and in judgments that emerge from a process of holding principles and particulars responsible to each other.

Such practices enact an ideal of inclusion that refuses both reductive unities and limiting dichotomies, seeking instead the generative possibilities in liberal arts of connection across difference. These are complex considerations and do not easily lead us to quick-fix solutions or conclusive answers, and certainly not to new ideologies to replace the old. That is all to the good. Thinking of the liberal arts as entailing arts of translation and connection on all levels challenges us in both small and large ways to remember that society exists "*in* transmission, *in* communication."

This, too, is a dream of commonality, one that aspires to include many people and cultures without insisting on homogenization.

CHAPTER THREE

TOWARD MORE INCLUSIVE WAYS OF THINKING

Human eyes gazed at each of all these forms of life and saw resemblance in difference—the core of metaphor, that which lies close to the core of poetry itself, the only hope for a humane civil life. The eye for likeness in the midst of contrast, the appeal to recognition, the association of thing to thing, spiritual fact with embodied form, begins here. And so begins the suggestion of multiple, many-layered rather than singular meanings, wherever we look, in the ordinary world....This impulse to enter, with other humans, through language, into the order and disorder of the world, is poetic at its root as surely as it is political at its root. Poetry and politics both have to do with description and with power.
—Adrienne Rich

We are interested in ways that fundamental concepts, usually locked into oppositional definitions and usages, can be fruitfully connected.

We offer the following sketch of key shifts in ways of knowing, gleaned from many sources and experiences, as both means and products of arts of translation. We find what has been thought before in differing contexts given renewed meaning in present critiques of traditions, reconfigurations of knowledge, emerging fields and subject areas. Here, we are interested in ways that fundamental concepts, usually locked into oppositional definitions and usages, can be fruitfully connected. The concepts we describe below can be understood as relating to and informing each other rather than as essentially oppositional. These kinds of newly generative connections are threads that interweave what we see and welcome in the emerging new academy.

In moving between the terms paired below, we are not suggesting going "from—to." We are recasting oppositions as generative tensions and so are focusing on polar terms as they mutually require each other, and on that which mediates them—relations, processes, mutual transactions. The polarities are then reframed not as oppositional but complementary, as sustaining the generativity of the tensions, or anchoring the ends of continua.

We are by no means claiming that what follows is brand new, or that it is adequately developed in this sketch. Rather, we suggest that what some have characterized as wars over liberal education indicates not only disagreements but, also, the emergence of something new. That something new comprises emerging reconfigurations of older and newer voices, ways of thinking, and subject areas that undo the conceptual grounds that have too often locked us into futile arguments.

In order to work on curricular, pedagogical, and institutional changes together, we believe it is wise, practical, and responsible to explore ways of thinking that reframe old problems. Again, in this time of exploring the relations of educational issues and aspirations for a more egalitarian democracy, it is important to think not only about what we are doing, but about how we are thinking.

Here, then, are some shifts in ways of thinking we discern and believe to be promising for a shared common quest to learn together with and from the resources of our differences.

UNIVERSAL/PARTICULAR

There is great emphasis today on undoing the universalizing of concepts, forms, standards, and prescriptive definitions that have previously anchored fields, theories, cultures, and polities. Ethnic studies and cultural studies locate and question universalized notions, such as definitions of what it means to be properly human, that stand in the way of fully respectful openness to humankind's diversities. Women's studies scholars question universalized notions of the qualities, activities, and achievements of man that were actually derived from and prescribed for a particular group of males, and thus were not generic or universal at all. Postmodern scholarship critiques notions of the self, literature, the state, and power in order to uncover fluid, complex, multiple meanings that are created and enacted in the small, everyday dealings of particular times and lives, rather than expressing essences or universals. Contemporary science proposes differing relations between order and chaos, stability and change, than those that shaped the modern Western consciousness and informed many of the dominant metaphors in all fields. Drawing on such creative critiques and the new scholarship for which they open space across once firm lines, we can search for differing modes of relationality and generalization derived from more varied sets of particulars, unconstrained by either the limitations or the exclusionary errors of past times.

Nevertheless, as universals are questioned from so many sides it can appear that nothing is left except particulars—about which, we may suddenly realize, nothing can then meaningfully be said. As Leonard Fein (1994) notes in writing about the question of "Jewish continuity," we inherit this postmodern problem from modernism because "modernity asserts that loyalties to groups smaller than the whole family of humankind are regressive; it endorses universalism and condemns particularism. But Judaism, however universalist it may be in ideology, has always been particular in structure." The same could be said, *mutatis mutandis*, about issues

16

of identity raised by modernist universality and "value-free" positivism for those in other religious and cultural frames, and, in fact, for specific academic fields as well. When particularity, or localized identities, are found to serve prejudice, to divide and cause conflict, or otherwise to block fruitful thinking, universalism (and/or value neutrality) seems to promise relief. But we cannot undo all particularity and its defining specific values without throwing out the baby of meaningfulness with the bathwater of prejudice and divisiveness. What would Judaism *be* if it did not have particular forms, methods, materials, symbols, rituals, logics, definitions, and if these were not reflective of value-directed choices? The same premise applies to Protestantism, or belief in the truth claims of modern Western science, or functional definitions of what is and what is not to be studied as literature. Absent particulars, how could we learn them if we did not have something to learn that is discernably not everything else we could also learn? But at the same time, they are not only particular. Is what is meant by the law of gravity, or a religious commandment, or a principle of justice entirely captured by any particular formulation or practice or experience or observation?

We begin to see that universals and particulars are related to each other in complex ways, and that we must now pay attention to how they are related rather than feel forced to choose one and give up the other. Fein, recalling Santayana, reminds us that "it is as foolish to suppose that one can be a human being in general as to suppose that one can speak language in general. Universalism and particularism are not mutually exclusive; they are complementary, and the ideal relationship between them is one of creative tension rather than head-on-head antagonism." We need not focus on radically "purified" definitions of abstract universals or unique particulars. *We can choose to refocus so that we also take account of all that actually mediates between these poles*. We can refocus on cultures and societies and organizations and groups and eras and peoples from and for which the abstractions of knowledge, the symbols and rituals of religions, the methods of sciences, and definitions of fields were and are derived in the first place. Such mediating terms allow us to imagine universal values beyond them by which they, being human and historical and therefore particular, can be evaluated and changed.

For example, can we understand a specific kind of work someone does without a universalized concept of work to which we refer? If not, the loss of the universalized idea would leave us helpless. But in fact we can. There are always multiple approaches still available. We can consider several different possible definitions of work developed at different times in differing societies, observe what some people say they think of as work when they do it, and reflect with others both inside and outside of our profes-

Can we understand a specific kind of work someone does without a universalized concept of work to which we refer?

17

sions about what we find. In this way we can think about what work can mean and be in particular situations without universalizing on the one hand or becoming lost in a welter of specific observations. Comparisons of conventional meanings and practices yield clearer general—not universal—ideas. Moreover, in being more particular and comparative, we can locate oddities—even injustices—in previously generalized or universalized definitions and studies which may have omitted important particulars. Leaders in academic fields, as in religions, cultures, and conceptions of science, have all done precisely that. There is no established set of human beliefs and practices that has not changed through the years as people have struggled to express their particular values and purposes in relation to generalizations.

Whether or not it is possible to find universals, then, surely any quest for them is better served by exploration of many particulars, many examples, multiple experiences and meanings, than by insistence that that which is known is already in its final form of expression. As in the examples above, too much emphasis on what some term has come to mean can, in fact, lead to a lack of awareness of perspectives and information that were not available to or were discounted or ignored by earlier scholars and practitioners.

Again, we are not forced to choose between universality or particularities. These are polar (and extremely abstract) notions. Between them lies a great deal that allows us to make useful, meaningful statements; to judge by adequate standards for reasonable purposes; to generalize while remaining open to new evidence, more voices.

Nor are we required to give up all universals because some have been proven to be in fact partial—as were the "ideal types," "rational" and "economic" "man," and "scientific" theories that "proved" the grounds for racism and sexism, and religious practices that expressed some peoples' failures of universalized love and justice. Universals may play a crucial role as aspirational notions, or horizons of thought, hope, and faith. Thus a notion of justice that is not conflated with any one set of laws keeps us responsibly critical of legal measures we enact, able to be proud of achievements but also always trying to do better. Similarly, an aspirational moral belief in the intrinsic worth of all people that coincides entirely with no culture's or religion's particular definitions and values can keep us listening to each other even when we encounter serious disagreements. To be grounded in one way need not, after all, require us to confuse that way with the mystery of all that it is a way to, or for: quite the contrary.

Surely any quest for universals is better served by exploration of many particulars than by insistence that that which is known is already in its final form of expression.

TIMELESS/HISTORICAL

The eternal and the temporal have been opposed in ways related and similar to the opposition of universal and particular, with a higher value ascribed to that which has been taken to be both universal and eternal. This seems so self-evident to many that it may appear odd even to notice it. It is, however, a particular position; in liberal education it is precisely such foundational assumptions we need to examine to achieve self-knowledge, and to explore others' positions, whether we then change or not. We can approach academic disciplines and multiple cultural traditions, as well as other ways of knowing, comparatively, locating them in their contexts and histories, to avoid thinking only in terms of any particular pre-ordained hierarchies. If no single system, principle, or set of standards is granted beforehand the position of unevaluated judge in sole possession of eternal truths and standards, we can engage in fruitful dialogues across many lines. As we come to know other cultures and their knowledge and faith traditions better, and as we also study the histories of established disciplines through which scholars have in the past sought such comparative knowledge, we will at the very least decrease the chances of serious misunderstandings—no small achievement, in fact.

In liberal as distinct from theological or ideological education, we can undertake to engage claims of possessing timeless truths and principles and methodologies as themselves historical, whatever else they may also be. For example, the field of religious studies was created as a subject appropriate to liberal education by scholars who were interested in religions as historical, philosophical, sociological, anthropological phenomena. Thus even subjects defined by claims of eternal and universal truths, some of which profoundly contradict each other, can be historicized and taught comparatively in ways that allow us to retain our differences yet increase in mutual understanding and respect. And religiously affiliated liberal arts schools can also teach truths they take to be necessarily eternal in ways that hold open the mystery of the connection between the universal/eternal and the particular/temporal. Students can comprehend religious identity defined in a particular way lovingly, respectfully, and therefore also critically. If one loves the eternal, one is obligated, after all, not to worship in its place the partialities of imperfect times and people.

It has been said that there is rational as well as religious idolatry, and that both have to do with confusing a partial, historical expression with the truth itself. In terms of most subject areas, this means most simply that, as feminist (Bleier 1984, Haraway 1989, Hubbard 1990, Keller 1985, Rosser 1994) and other critical scholars (Foucault 1973, Kuhn 1970) have shown for the history of science, there are many factors that have always been involved in the contestations through which some knowledge is pursued, some rejected, some established, some forgotten. And telling the stories of knowledge creation, past and present, need not reduce it to a function of its times. On the contrary: historicizing quite literally hu-

It has been said that there is rational as well as religious idolatry, and that both have to do with confusing a partial, historical expression with the truth itself.

manizes scholarship, and so makes it more equitably accessible as an activity those previously alienated from it can think of joining. And as more of us continue to enter the worlds of scholarship and education, the knowledge we receive, work with, challenge, and create also becomes more capacious. Ironically, by reducing the claims of present knowledge to be above time and place and culture, we may increase the likelihood that future knowledge, and with it future understandings and practices of egalitarian democracies, will indeed have a larger reach.

CENTRAL/MARGINAL

Searching for particular, historical, contextual grounds and stories of what has been claimed to be universal and eternal allows us to locate ways and places in which unjustifiable claims to such absoluteness have been made. Thus we clear the ground for respectful exploration of that which was marginalized and/or hidden by faulty conceptions. When, for example, one culture's particular definitions of art are absolutized, claimed to be universal and nonhistorical, the creations of other people within and outside of that culture come to be marginalized, defined as nonart, perhaps as "merely" craft, or "primitive." Or when what is "normal" is defined in male gendered terms, and/or in Western terms, but is presented as centrally, universally normal, the majority of humankind can only be seen as deviant, even abnormal.

The point, however, is not to fight over who, or what, *is* central, or *is* marginal, but to see those positionings in their contexts rather than as absolute. There may always be centers and margins, but there can also always be many centers and many margins that change places depending on time, purpose, contexts, interests, needs, values, and differentials in access to power. Seeing center and margin as in transaction rather than as static opposites allows us to reconfigure relations, to move margin to center and vice versa and see what that reveals about both—and the in-between as well. We can then see, for example, how what Toni Morrison (1992) calls the "africanist presence" in the United States has always been marginalized and therefore is foundationally implicated in the dominant, central white culture. That which is defined as central requires a margin, is dependent on that marginalizing. Similarly, American Indians in differing but interrelated ways have also thus been made central to non-native "American" identities.

Definitions of what constitutes in theory and in particularized practices "significant" knowledge, "proper" citizenship, "true" spirituality, "high" culture, "qualified" and "desirable" faculty members and students tend, of course, to hold in place what has been taken to be central and to perpetuate old marginalizations and devaluations. What is in question again today, as it has repeatedly been in the course of human history, is not whether centering is good or bad, but whether, when, and how such focusing reflects, not appropriate judgments, but rather old prejudices that narrow the range of possible knowledge and action for all.

Thus, to take a contemporary example, we also need not polarize positions as for or against affirmative action. Affirmative action is not an absolute, nor is its opposite some set of purely "objective" criteria for judging by "merit" alone. Affirmative action is a historically specific and still changing set of strategies designed to counter deeply entrenched and still potent racist and sexist systems that, even after the Civil Rights Act, inequitably limited access to central positions. It is, in this sense, new. Yet insofar as it expresses complex identity and value choices made by academic institutions aware of their responsibilities to the broader polity as well as their own particular missions, it is by no means unprecedented. Factors of balance, representation, and recognition of special contributions brought by particular groups of people have always played a role in academic selectivity. Schools that wish to move from being regionally to being nationally defined act affirmatively to recruit and select students from underrepresented areas. Schools that are building their reputations in the arts seek and affirmatively recruit students and faculty members in the area they wish to strengthen. Sports-oriented schools act affirmatively to bring in athletes. Religiously affiliated schools give preference to, or require, adherence to their faith traditions—or, if they desire greater diversity, on the contrary seek out people from other traditions. Schools that have strong reputations in the humanities sometimes choose to act affirmatively to recruit scientists. And in all such instances, institutions make great efforts to provide those they are seeking to attract and to hold with what they require. Most of these practices are generally seen as benign practices of self-definition and institutional development. Diversifying in the ways now specifically called affirmative action expresses the choice to become more just, more truthful, and more interestingly varied.

However, enforcement of antiprejudicial practices at many institutions that would not otherwise have chosen diversification as one of their own goals has upset some people. They see it as a new and alien intrusion of "preferential" treatment—as if educational institutions had never exercised value-driven selectivity by categories before. Equalizing access is not the same as granting unfair privilege. It is required precisely because the effects of unfair privilege are locked into definitions of who and what has in the past been defined as central. We believe that a national effort to undo national failures of justice is fully justified in educational institutions committed to excellence (as distinct from prejudice-defined exclusivity) in a country aspiring to live up to the commitment to "liberty and justice for all."

Affirmative action is not an absolute, nor is its opposite some set of purely "objective" criteria for judging by "merit" alone.

Not long ago, there were quotas that limited the number of Jews, of women, of people of color, of particular immigrant groups, and so we have needed countermeasures. But we are not thereby absolutizing the countermeasures, saying that target percentages or carefully scrutinized rectificatory procedures are of themselves and for all time good. Nor are we saying that the hitherto marginalized shall now and for all time be central.

What/who is central and what/who is marginal are related to each other, and to times, contexts, purposes, and aspirations. Ethnic studies programs and women's studies and the other reconfigurations of the new academy, supported by various kinds of affirmative action, move differing issues to the center in order to help us move from prejudice—prejudgment—to more careful, responsible, and appropriate judgments. As we move among them, focusing and refocusing from margins to centers, we prepare to comprehend ourselves and each other as different, yes, but not as radically unrelated or immutably hierarchically ranked. We begin to see our mutual implications, the ways centrality is defined by marginality and vice versa, and hence also our mutual responsibilities, defined in more ethically and intellectually adequate ways. As with universals and particulars, the eternal and the temporal, it is how centers and margins have been, are, should be, and could be related rather than statically ranked and opposed that calls for our critical, creative attention.

HUMAN/KIND OF HUMAN

All of the above helps us in efforts to undo centuries of constructions of what it means to be human that created kinds of humans, some of whom were defined as being less properly, fully, adequately human in desperately dangerous and absurdly false ways. There may be commonalities among all humans, and there may be kinds of humans: these remain, always, to be studied, thought about, explored. We are by no means all alike individually or in various groupings. We need to understand our differences, and the differences between and among those never equalized differences as well, discerning what may be given and what is historically constructed. We are convinced, however, that such work proceeds far more accurately than often it has in the past when we do not begin with assumptions that mark some of us as permanent occupants of a centralized, universalized humanness and others of us as marginalized particular kinds to be measured against the very standards that have been used to justify exclusion—as not so long ago it was held that women could not be educated because, unlike men, women's reproductive capacities required them not to think "too much."

If, as a key example, being rational is indeed a defining characteristic of humans, then not only are all humans fundamentally rational, but the modes and forms of rationality may well be far more fascinatingly complex than millennia of narrow, hierarchical definitions and their necessarily inadequate standards of judgment of what is and what is not proper or good reasoning have allowed us all to know. New research is enlarging our understanding of "women's ways of knowing" (Belenky et al. 1986), differing "frames of mind" (Gardener 1983), and disparate cultures' logics, narrative forms, and modes of persuasion and discovery. As these differing ways of thinking, knowing, and learning are brought forward for our attention, we can reconfigure relations between and among these human modes and expressions. It is not, for example, necessary to think of emotions as utterly nonrational or irrational. Insofar as we are aware of them, emotions, too, are in their ways conceptual, and can be more or less accurate, informed, communicative, or privatized. It is necessary, too, for us to remember that the human mind is embodied, and that, in a constant interchange, we communicate through our bodies with others and with the world.

As we undo old prejudices that proclaimed some kinds of us primarily "body," and/or capable of emotion but not of reason, we also undo justifications used by others who defined themselves as more properly and purely rational—and so justified in maintaining themselves as "head" of the family, "head" of state, bringer of "enlightenment" to "primitive" peoples. We can then proceed to rethink meanings of rationality, emotion, and body to comprehend what they may mean as distinguishable but relational aspects of a fully articulated humanness in which potentially we all share equally.

It is useful to remember that individuality is itself a particular historical notion.

INDIVIDUAL/COMMUNITY

In this country, centered as it is on notions about individuality, it is useful to remember that individuality is itself a particular historical notion that developed in specific contexts and that it has created some problems even as it has solved others. There are cultures in which the idea that one can be a separate individual is almost inconceivable, and that, too, solves some problems and creates others. It is possible to learn from both, and to think of individuals-in-community. Community can be seen as having meaning with and through individuals while at the same time individuals find meaning with and through community. These, too, are terms that can be distinguished and yet understood to be mutually created and implicated in such a way that we do not enforce the submission of one to the other.

Nor does each term occupy a fixed position. For example, the dominant tradition in the West has developed a profoundly important legal and political as well as intellectual emphasis on the concept of the rights-bearing individual. But necessary as the tradition of individual rights is to counter both individual- and group-directed injustices, the concept of the

The relative weights

of individuality,

communality,

and ascribed social

grouping do not remain

fixed over time.

rights of collectivities is also, today, under consideration. As in the notion of class action suits, it is reasonable under some circumstances to treat individuals as members of a group when harm done has affected them categorically. In hate crimes, targeted individuals are attacked not for any individual action or quality, but for their ascribed group membership. Where such categories remain persistently and seriously potent, they have effects that may have to be countered on the level they actually work: against groups. Thus, political theorists such as Iris Marion Young (1990) suggest that, "To promote social justice…social policy should sometimes accord special treatment to groups." She then explores, as examples raised by recent social movements, "pregnancy and birthing rights for workers, bilingual-bicultural rights, and American Indian rights."

These are hotly contested issues. Absolutized and lifted out of all temporal contexts, the principle of individual rights may seem utterly incompatible with rights of groups. To avoid unproductive oppositions, it helps to remember here, too, that the relative weights of individuality, communality, and ascribed social grouping do not remain fixed over time. Sometimes one, sometimes another is more central or more marginal to a particular situation. We need to take particular situations into account to help us discern when justice is best served by stressing individuality or group concerns, holding both in mind as factors and sources of possible principled action. Such discernment or practical judgement is supported by the realization that individuals always exist in relation, and that there are many mediating systems between the individual and the state that are also relevant to justice as to identity issues.

Absolutized principles are important, we repeat, as horizons, as aspirations and guides, but we live in a particular world to which absolutized principles must be applied with respect for realities.

Along these lines, many in the United States are exploring what Carol Gilligan (1982), Nell Nodding (1984), Sara Ruddick (1989), and others call "an ethic of care," grounded in obligations of dependencies, nurturance, and relationships. Legal scholars, political philosophers, ethicists, psychologists, and others are working to understand how we can take into account not only the rights and responsibilities pertaining to public life— long defined in contradistinction to private life, to which women and disenfranchised men were assigned—but also the obligations and rightful expectations of care. There are, of course, other cultures and subcultures that have long centered on the primacy of relationships, sometimes to such an extent that individual rights cannot be well recognized. Here, too, it is not necessary that we choose between one pole or the other. We can learn from both, and, recognizing the tensions between them, press forward our efforts to treat both individuals and groups as worthy of understanding and respect even as we must, at times, take particular stands.

In all these ways, liberal learning is reshaping itself, creating new modes of thought as well as new subject matters. Reconfigurations of knowledge, creative critiques of once dominant traditions, and shifts in focus emerge from the new academy as it grows up from, around, and in the interstices of the old.

We propose, indeed we urge, that in our conversations and in our class-rooms, we draw on these reshapings to move beyond polarities and the combative relations they create.

Refusing dichotomies, we can practice the liberal arts of translation:

- developing respectful comparisons and contrasts;

- making dialogical connections;

- risking tentative but responsible judgments; and

- creating ever-changing syntheses that illuminate and sometimes make it possible to transcend static, polarized oppositions.

This does not mean that we cover over, ignore, or in any way trivialize oppositions and the struggles they have always created where we genuinely differ about important matters. It does mean that we can, if we will, practice shifting modes of thinking and arts of translation that may help us better educate our students for a world characterized by multiplicities, intricate relations, and change.

CHAPTER FOUR

A RENEWAL OF EDUCATIONAL COMMITMENTS

Democracy…is a community always in the making. If educators hold this in mind, they will remember that democracy is forever incomplete: it is founded in possibilities. Even in the small, the local places in which teaching is done, educators may begin creating the kinds of situations where, at the very least, students will begin telling the stories of what they are seeking, what they know and might not yet know, exchanging stories with others grounded in other landscapes, at once bringing something into being that is in-between….
It is at moments like these that persons begin to recognize each other and, in the experience of recognition, feel the need to take responsibility for each other.
—Maxine Greene

It is time to reframe and renew our commitments as educators for a democracy "still in the making," to address historically developed diversities, human differences, relations, and change. We call, therefore, for the following five interrelated educational commitments:

• an exploration of *grounded selves*, enabled by understanding of self and others, to enter into

• *relational pluralism*, pluralism redefined, reassessed, and given meaning and particular purpose by

• *contextualized knowing and knowledge*, that informs developing capacities for

• mutually respectful *dialogues among cultures and multiple meaning systems*, in the context and for the sake of

• *fully participatory democracies*.

These are proposed as suggestive themes for liberal education, emphases that help us continue practicing arts of thinking and living together. In different times, there were other framings of the liberal arts. Our framings, too, are particular, historical, evolving.

GROUNDED SELVES

We do not enter education or civic life as blank slates.

Today people are once again discussing the limitations of an abstract notion of the individual in order to explore instead "the self-in-relation," "the individual-in-communities," individuals and communities relating to the state through mediating systems of many kinds. At the same time, we note, some are also interested in contextualizing and historicizing notions of communities, so that we do not trade the abstract individual for an equally abstract collectivity. As multicultural histories of the United States, such as that of Ronald Takaki (1993) and Fiol-Matta and Chamberlain's anthology (1994) make clear, United States culture has always been not just plural but interwoven. Our selves, like and with our cultures and this nation, are already multicultural, as, indeed, are our languages and many of our most familiar cultural forms. None of us is single, impermeable, immutable, unrelated, or unaffected by overlapping influences that provide us with varying kinds of interconnected common grounds.

We do not enter education or civic life as blank slates, or as singular representatives of any one kind of person, culture, or age. The social and cultural communities that are uniquely configured in each of us connect us even as they distinguish us. Insofar as we leave our various connections unexplored, we find ourselves with students who may indeed seem to be blank slates—a cruel error—or who, having to retrieve their identities from our neglect, do not trust us to engage with them at all.

When we undo the absoluteness of the idea of fundamentally separate selves meeting on supposedly neutral ground in order to learn together, we can more readily see how it is appropriate to concern ourselves in liberal education with developing democratic arts of associative living.

Inviting our students and colleagues to be more fully present, we encounter the same needs for such arts as we have in civic life. We have to learn how to relate across our differences, and to be able to converse by more than one set of norms.

RELATIONAL PLURALISM

When we begin with grounded selves, interpersonal, community-nurtured, culturally and cross-culturally informed *relations* become recognized aspects of our identities. In this way atomistic pluralism can be transformed into *relational* pluralism. We become able to think of this nation not as an aggregation of isolated individuals, but as itself both grounded in and aspiring to a more equitable interconnectedness among people. Just as the concept of relational pluralism enables us to move forward the relations among people, it also emphasizes links among groups or communities that may have thought of themselves and been thought of as cut off from other collectivities defined in isolation from each other.

Privatizing culture ("Your culture is your own business") in order to "protect" supposedly culturally neutral civic practices from the challenges of dealing with differing cultures is no solution. There is no preexisting, nonhistorically particular, neutral common public ground from the perspective of which Americans can lump together indiscriminately all those "different others" with their ethnic cultures as if they were the problem, and not equally part of the United States. To privatize culture is to silence some and perpetuate the privilege of others. On the other hand, privileging cultures to such an extent that we forget to struggle with issues of shared public life and mutual political responsibility across community and cultural boundaries is equally problematic. It locks us all variously into the past, turns cultures into constraints, and so forces us into negotiating, at best, across defended boundaries. This is precisely the model of political life we are attempting to reconfigure with the concept of grounded selves and the relational pluralism that concept makes conceivable.

Our curricula as well as our pedagogy must avoid two threatening extremes. On the one hand, there is concern that culture may replace the individual as the basic player in civic life. Concentrating only on one's identity with a given group threatens to lead to the degeneration of relational pluralism into a nation marked by discontinuities and divisions. On the other hand, as relational pluralists we must remain vigilant lest differences be erased and whole communities become, once again, invisible in education and public life.

As always, we need not choose between polarized positions. Relational pluralism helps us remember that selves, communities, and cultures are differing but not radically divided, that they are ways of focusing on who we are that change from being central to being marginal at different times.

In this context, we critique educational responses to diversity that effectively conflate societies in Asia, Africa, Latin America, and elsewhere as if they were interchangeable, for curricular purposes, with the multiple communities and social identities that comprise United States relational pluralism. Our students do indeed need knowledge of world cultures and of the roots of United States cultures in more disparate world sources than have heretofore been admitted or studied. They also need sophisticated knowledge about the cultures, communities, relations, and fallible traditions that now comprise their own societies. We cannot assign them to study medieval China or African art and believe that they are then prepared to address the diversities in their own neighborhoods, classrooms, campuses. In the United States as elsewhere, there is no one "real" culture from the perspective of which all others become the same in being

Relational pluralism helps us remember that selves, communities, and cultures are differing but not radically divided.

different from it—and hence equally available to diversify it. Furthermore, not all differences have been equally weighted. It has not, for example, historically been the same to be European American as it has to be African American, or Mexican American, and these have not been the same as being American Indian—nor are all American Indians the same.

To engage liberal learning with issues of diversity, multiculturalism, and international cultures will therefore require more than a multicultural course requirement that can be filled from a list to which present departments can add anything they like. It requires more than the presence of international studies, more than "dots of diversity" in syllabi, more than women's studies and a few ethnic studies programs on campus. All of these are needed, and none of them ought to be out of conversation with the others, or with the professionalized academic disciplines. It is fruitful, translational conversations we need, not a bit of this and a dollop of that.

We encourage, then, courageous exploration of how, in public life as in education, we can together face directly the challenges posed by our historically unequalized diversities as well as our multiple cultural differences. We need neither be melted in the same pot, nor made as much as possible the same, nor held utterly separate to be equal. Meaningful equality, which disrupts old divided and hierarchical constructions of our many ways of being human, allows the many forms of our relational pluralism to enrich, rather than fragment, a shared civic life.

CONTEXTUALIZING AND HISTORICIZING KNOWERS AND KNOWLEDGE

Selves, communities, cultures, and public practices defined as grounded in their multiple relations and histories cannot, by definition, be studied or comprehended in isolation from their overlapping contexts and their roots in times and places. The self of the knower, the scholar, the student, the teacher is no longer as likely to be utterly (actually, impossibly) banished as if it were always necessarily a source of contagion to "purely" objective, impartial knowledge. Instead, historical, cultural contexts are openly present to be responsibly evaluated. We need not fear reductionism. Holding ideals of objectivity in tension with their correlative, subjectivity, one can study the times in which a particular scholar wrote to help interpret his/her work. Remembering contexts and times, centers and margins, one can also focus on what is said as it is framed by what is omitted, on who appears and who could have, but doesn't. By telling a fuller story about what and whom we teach, we return the world to scholarship, making it possible for more of our very diverse students to see connections to themselves, their own worlds, and those of others.

We see many results from this renewed turn to histories, relationality, and contexts. Consider, for example, the striking biographies of philosophers: Monk's (1990) biography of Wittgenstein, Miller's (1993) of

Foucault, Young-Bruehl's (1982) of Arendt, and the philosophical–cultural essays of Anthony Appiah, *In My Father's House* (1992). These studies place their subjects and their philosophizing within their times so that philosophy is made more human, more accessible, more evidently relevant to civic concerns of many kinds. Stuart Hampshire (1989), a philosopher of ethics, begins one of his books by telling about his own background so that the reader is aware that philosophers, like all of us, make choices that are informed by particular lives and values. Scholarship can thus be seen as an act of commitment intrinsically related to public and moral actions.

Similar developments are visible in virtually all fields. Stories of knowledge seeking are brought forward rather than withheld as somehow contaminating, reductive, or just inappropriate. As a result, the relations of all of liberal learning to engaged citizenship are becoming significantly easier to comprehend and to demonstrate.

In moving contexts forward, we also prepare to question more or less unspoken assumptions that there are absolute, ahistorical, context-free warrants and justifications for knowledge. There may or may not be such warrants. Or, there may be such warrants in some fields, in some ways, and not in others. The point is to explore such foundational claims openly, holding these issues of the timeless and temporal in tension. Such open engagement with the claims made by knowledge, meaning, and value systems gives us practice in judging claims for ourselves, rather than being prejudiced in favor of those that make the most familiar or most sweeping claims. It has often been suggested, after all, that there is a particular historical context for the belief that being ahistorical is either possible or desirable. This history too should be evaluated.

In this spirit, we admire revised versions of "Western Civilization" courses that are more complex and multivocal than those that once claimed to teach "The Story of Civilization," or to trace "The Ascent of Man," as if all peoples and all cultures through all of time could be subsumed into one teleological story of progress. That a culture would tell its own story in such a way is itself something to examine. Liberal education ought to help us learn how to learn about vastly differing civilizations, not teach us how to judge all by the standards of any one.

Obviously, we are interested, not worried, by the notion that knowledge is human artifact informed by the interests, commitments, assumptions and values of particular, historical, culturally embedded (not determined) knowers. But we are clear that this need not mean that knowledge becomes indistinguishable from bias or opinion. Between the absolutized poles of prejudice and disinterestedness, or the subjective and the objective, lies the view that knowledge is always a mixture of individual inten-

Liberal education ought to help us learn how to learn about vastly differing civilizations, not teach us how to judge all by the standards of any one.

tions and choices; historical, social, and cultural meanings; and particular formalized knowledge traditions and communities.

Knowledge is already held responsible to its contemporary professionalized academic communities' standards. For all of the above reasons, we believe it should also be responsible to the communities that in a full sense surround, inform, and support specialization—and specialists. As Cornel West (1993) has put it, we encourage liberal education for "engaged intellectuals" who deal openly with the realization that scholarship, teaching, and learning profoundly matter, because they draw from and have effects on communities far beyond the academic professions.

To venture forth from the too aptly named ivory tower in order to enter purposefully into broader conversations and to accept responsibility for both scholarly and public effects of our work is scary, but it is not necessarily to submit to inappropriate pressures, to taint or skew knowledge. It is possible to take many considerations into account and yet maintain integrity, whether we do so as scholars, teachers, or citizens. Taking on the challenge of understanding and practicing how to sustain integrity in the face of complexity is one of the goals we see for the new academy.

DIALOGUES AMONG DIFFERENCES

Some fear that coming to know ourselves as grounded, relational creatures of particular times and places, and historicizing systems of meaning, might further separate us. We do, after all, differ and some of our differences are genuinely incompatible. What will happen, then, if we do not declare some grounds neutral, universal rather than particular?

We believe that the kind of regrounding we describe may make unproductive conflict less, not more, likely. By focusing on relationalities through multiplicities and change, such reframings help keep us from locking into the kind of unchanging, absolutized positions that leave few options but conflict when anyone differs or dissents. They also help us equalize participants in dialogues by teaching us to refuse any group's unexamined claims to possess the only acceptable neutral, common ground. We can, then, make creating common grounds a project we undertake together in ways that are appropriate to differing situations, groups, purposes. Mutually respectful exploration of many perspectives can be, quite simply, so interesting that the sheer pleasure of learning can predispose people to work together toward shared understandings and new kinds of syntheses.

Engaging in cross-cultural discussions invites critical examination not only of differing meaning systems, but of what it means to compare. The Chicago Cultural Studies group observes that, "One could say that universals only emerge out of comparisons and cannot be grounded except through radical comparisons; and while this comparison may resemble the

32

effort to coordinate local perspectives from a transcendent standpoint, the difference is that radical comparison cannot presuppose that it will finally produce any universals. It may just [but note that it may indeed] produce a set of linkages."

Further, by engaging in dialogues across differences in a reflective, critical mode, we also prepare to exercise uncertain but responsible judgment informed by increasingly knowledgeable empathy. Kant, in *The Critique of Judgment*, called for development of "the enlarged mentality" by which we become more able to think coherently for ourselves because we can also "think in the place of others." Conceiving of possibilities beyond those readily available to us in whatever communities we have been living and learning not only adds to our thinking; it helps us do it better. We believe many fields can benefit from the virtues of the mode of thought of which Merleau-Ponty wrote: "Ethnology…is a way of thinking, the way which imposes itself when the object is 'different,' and requires us to transform ourselves. We also become the ethnologists of our own society if we set ourselves at a distance from it."

Committing ourselves to dialogue, we no longer merely tolerate the differences of others, nor do we indiscriminately "celebrate diversity," but engage with each other and with multiple works and cultures in a quest for mutual illumination. We are then able to seek comprehension such that no one and no group is either appropriated and absorbed by those who "include" them, nor is devalued, exoticized, or "othered." Knowing becomes more transactional.

Such an approach to other cultures (and our own) is premised on mutuality rather than predetermined hierarchy. It involves practicing the relational arts of thinking. Through dialogues among differences we not only gain in knowledge of other cultures and people, but also realize that we do not have to prescribe beforehand a single common ground to which all "proper" knowers, all "acceptable" citizens, all "good" students must submit. Rather, we remember that, with practice, we can indeed comprehend each other across the differences we bring with us. It is possible, after all, to listen to a deductive argument, a preacher's exhortation, a poetic image, a citation of fact, an emotionally expressive outburst, a story from a still unfamiliar culture—and to make some sense of them all. At such times, one's own understanding is stretched, challenged, enriched, as are one's own abilities to think and speak in many ways. We thus create a common ground of understanding as we think and speak together, rather than setting rules for entrance beforehand so that only those willing and able to act as if they were alike can enter, or succeed.

Committing ourselves to dialogue, we engage with each other and with multiple works and cultures in a quest for mutual illumination.

PARTICIPATORY DEMOCRACY

Educational institutions can serve as middle grounds where the skills of participatory democracy can be practiced.

When we hear people today refer anxiously to the proliferation of interest and identity groups in the nation and on our campuses, we are reminded of Alexis de Tocqueville's observation that the United States he visited was characterized by a truly remarkable number and variety of groups and associations. Despite his aristocratic fears of the "leveling" effect of democracy and its potential for chaos, what he saw was not a mass of isolated, hostile individuals but a nation in which people joined together for all sorts of purposes.

Things have changed since Tocqueville visited, of course, but as Evans and Boyte (1986) observe, how we come together and with whom still matters a great deal. They write,

> In present day America recognition of both the centrality and the limitations of communities assumes no small urgency. Where are the places in our culture through which people sustain bonds and history? What are the processes through which they may broaden their sense of the possible, make alliances with others, develop the practical skills and knowledge to maintain democratic organizations? What are the languages of protest, dissent, and change that express moral and communal themes in inclusive ways that reach beyond particular boundaries of race, ethnicity, gender, and class?

These are crucial questions for liberal education that claims to prepare students to participate fully as democratic citizens. We find resources to respond to them in the new academy. When we focus on contexts, histories, and our multiple interrelations through them, practicing arts of translation of many kinds, we also prepare ground for the democratic virtues of open-mindedness and creativity.

Evans and Boyte call to our attention what we can learn from "democratic movements, drawing their spirit from voluntary associations of all sorts, [that] have not only sought structural changes to realize a wider, more inclusive and participatory 'democracy'…[but have] also illustrated the inextricable links between participation and citizenship." They cite, for example, "the commonwealth vision of the WCTU, the Knights of Labor, and the nineteenth-century Populists," as well as "the Citizenship Schools of the Southern Christian Leadership Conference in the 1960s and the citizenship education programs in community groups today." In these movements and the "free spaces" they create, differing people practice thinking, speaking, learning, and acting together. From such particular experiences of relational pluralism, they emerge with skills that help them continue to take part in civic actions. People's movements like these suggest models for ways educational institutions can serve as culturally complex middle grounds where the skills of participatory democracy can be learned and practiced.

Too often, democracy and democratic pluralism are taken as givens—not as hard-won, historically situated, painfully imperfect by their own highest values, and always still in negotiation both in this country and internationally. If we comprehended and were willing to act on what freedom, equality, and democracy as aspirational ideals translated into actual practices require of us, diversity would not be a problem today. Since it is indeed seen as a problem, we must engage, as educators, with efforts to face, analyze, and undo the past failures of our ideals this reveals, drawing on many resources, including, as suggested above, the history of peoples' movements.

The history of education in the United States has always reflected and influenced struggles over who is to govern, what equality requires of us, and how we are to engage in public life together justly. As education is also reconceived as requiring and providing "safe spaces" for many more of us, it becomes not a retreat from "real life" for a preselected few to prepare to lead "the many," but a location for practice of genuinely democratic arts of associative living and collaborative learning.

Still, some of those who are today proudly claiming membership in groups that have historically been marked as different are insisting on their own unified nature and on their separation from other groups. Is it not they, some ask, who are refusing the struggle for shared, equal public life in a fully participatory democracy? Are we not being divided by a strange kind of resegregation in ways that violate relational pluralism and the fully participatory democracy it grounds? Would it not be better, if this is so, to eliminate those segments of the new academy currently providing the safe spaces to which members of these groups repair?

There is indeed a danger of falling from a false unity that masked inequalities and differences into an equally paralyzing chaos of culturally defined and competing groups. But those who insist on studying their own community identities and histories need not be seen as creating divisive lines among us. Such work involves facing the fact that those lines are already present, and that we need to rescue, comprehend and value erased histories and cultures so that they, too, may become sources of knowledge and enrichment. In doing so, we correct terrible old errors, retrieve and express truths, visions, experiences, works, and values from which we can all learn. Separation can provide the spaces for work from which all will benefit.

We believe, then, that the programs and courses of study that have grown up in and around the old academy, necessitated by its exclusions, are crucial to the effort to revise liberal learning so that it will indeed pre-

People from virtually all fields are creating the new academy, and their work has affected their "home" disciplines as well.

pare us better for democratic practices. These programs should not now be dissolved out of fear of separateness in the name of mainstreaming. While we are indeed insistent on the importance of working together across boundaries, we do not believe we can rush past the time of focusing on particular cultures, untold or unfaced histories. If colleges and universities do not support "special studies," who will produce the knowledge that we need to enrich all courses? Who will provide homes on campus for those who are yet to be fully or genuinely welcomed? Who will keep up the pressure on a very long and powerful tradition that, left alone, will perpetuate its historical errors of exclusion, misinterpretation, devaluation? It is not "ghettoizing" a subject to provide it with an institutional home. On the contrary, it is, as with all discipline-based departments, providing for the safety, continuity, and scholarly community that makes good scholarship, teaching, and learning possible.

It is important to recognize, however, that the department-based disciplines are also engaged in creating an academy that more effectively educates us for participatory democracy. People from virtually all fields are creating the new academy, and their work has affected their "home" disciplines as well. Those disciplines, too, are reconfiguring as a result of such translation.

As subjects emerge, develop and establish themselves, they can become professionalized spheres of expertise ever more out of touch with other professions, let alone broader communities. There is nothing wrong with the intellectual development of fields into specialties; on the contrary, that is how knowledge boundaries are expanded, insights pressed to their conclusion, methods honed and methodologies reflected upon. But it becomes problematic if academic fields are not challenged also to maintain connections with the society that supports and needs its educated citizens. Education must not become a self-perpetuating enclave of particular kinds of professionals separated from each other and from civic life and its pressing concerns. This tendency must be regularly interrupted if our institutions are to prepare students for participation in a society that is continuing to commit itself to democracy. Newly emerging fields serve this function; they interrupt and revivify older ones. These developments are healthy for the academy and renewing for society.

DEMOCRATIC LIBERAL LEARNING

Liberal learning today as always involves positions on what counts as knowledge, what it means to be human, what social orders are and should be. Thus, today's active, multivocal discussions about the meanings of the liberal arts and their realization through curricula, pedagogies, and institutional structures *matter*. They are about books and subjects, yes, and they are also about ideals in tension with entrenched realities of power. That is why as educators we must care about racism and racialization, sexism, homophobia, class barriers, anti-Semitism, and all other expressions of the failures of aspirational democracy. These are failures of mind as much as they are failures of heart. They have infected epistemologies as well as practices of justice, because what we think and think we know has everything to do with the ways we make judgments and choices, the ways we act, and the systems we establish. What counts as literature, art, philosophy, music, science, and what is considered insignificant or unsound is decided in those systems, by those epistemologies. Who speaks and who is not heard; what is studied and what is neglected; who is supported and who is devalued as a result of such decisions and practices affect the future of this country as it continues to be shaped by and to shape its educational institutions.

Where discussion and exploration among many is not only welcomed but centrally valued in a democratic spirit, no particular substantive positions can be established as unchallengeable beforehand. Despite our endorsement of developments in contemporary scholarship and teaching, we continue to believe that there is no one correct, timeless definition of the liberal arts.

What we are proposing is that *liberal learning for our moment in history* is specifically challenged to help us learn how to cross borders and boundary lands, how to work across and with the resources of all our differences in our immediate as well as most extensive contexts. This is a challenge that has already proven its profound and exciting significance in reconfiguring liberal learning. How it will develop and change remains to be seen—and is up to all of us, and those who join and succeed us.

As we move on and off, around and through our changing, less insular campuses on both established and newer paths made by our many colleagues and students, we are being challenged to learn how to sustain multiple and even competing commitments. To do so, we are called to

Liberal learning for our moment in history is specifically challenged to help us learn how to cross borders and boundary lands.

develop our own value systems while honoring those of others, and—difficult as it is—to practice making consequential choices while recognizing significant disagreements. There are no guarantees that we will, in our differing ways, meet these challenges well, or even that we will ever agree on just what they are. But liberal education and the liberal arts today have already changed. They are no longer the preserve of a privileged few. They are also already more than the competitive marketplace of unrelated courses which educational leaders have decried for nearly two decades.

As we reconfigure what constitutes liberal education and strive for greater inclusiveness and equity, we generate new resources for once again engaging, for our times, crucial questions about how we are to live and learn together. It is these questions, and the responses being made to them in the new academy, that are shaping a liberal education for which diversity is indeed a resource, not a problem.

Let us, then, continue to discuss together how we can

- be reflective about ways of thinking that do and do not help us move beyond old divisions, oppositions, and hierarchies;

- include the subjects and competencies of the new academy as they help us reconfigure the liberal arts in order to engage them more fully with the quest for an open, common civic life;

- purposefully seek to develop the arts of translation, the abilities, commitments, and knowledges required to move respectfully among subjects and fields, individuals, communities, cultures, and nations;

- practice with our students and colleagues democratic arts of associative living, acting, and learning;

- make more permeable in both directions the boundaries between town and gown;

- teach and structure our institutions so that we and our students become both more grounded and able fully to recognize each other so that we may welcome our mutual responsibilities to each other and the world we share; and

- through such efforts, continue to try to live up to our claim that liberal education has as one of its fundamental purposes preparing students for lives as active citizens in a country still aspiring to democracy in an increasingly interdependent but hardly yet equitable world.

WORKS CITED

Appiah, Anthony. 1992. *In my father's house: Africa in the philosophy of culture*. London: Methuen.

Association of American Colleges and Universities. 1995. *The drama of diversity and democracy: Higher education and American commitments*. Washington, D.C.: Association of American Colleges and Universities.

Belenky, Mary Field, Blythe McVicker Clinchy, Nancy Rule Goldberger, and Jill Mattuck Tarule. 1986. *Women's ways of knowing: The development of self, voice, and mind*. New York: Basic Books.

Bleier, Ruth. 1984. *Science and gender: A critique of biology and its theories on women*. Elmsford, N.Y.: Pergamon Press.

Chicago Cultural Studies Group. 1992. Critical multiculturalism. In *Critical Inquiry* 18.

Cone, James. 1993. Martin and Malcolm, a dream or a nightmare? The Loy H. Witherspoon Lectures in Religious Studies, University of North Carolina–Charlotte.

Dewey, John. 1966. Reprint. *Democracy and education: An introduction to the philosophy of education*. New York: The Free Press. Original edition, New York: Macmillan, 1916.

Evans, Sara M., and Harry C. Boyte. 1986. *Free spaces: The sources of democratic change in America*. New York: Harper and Row.

Fein, Leonard. 1994. *Smashing idols and other prescriptions for Jewish continuity*. New York: The Nathan Cummings Foundation.

Fiol-Matta, Liza, and Mariam K. Chamberlain, eds. 1994. *Women of color and the multicultural curriculum*. Old Westbury, N.Y.: The Feminist Press.

Flax, Jane. 1990. Postmodernism and gender relations in feminist theory. In *Feminism/Postmodernism*. Edited by Linda J. Nicholson. New York: Routledge.

Foucault, Michel. 1973. Reprint. *The order of things: An archaeology of the human sciences*. New York: Vintage Books/Random House. Originally published as *Les mots et les choses*, Paris: Gallimard, 1966.

Gardener, Howard. 1983. *Frames of mind: The theory of multiple intelligences*. New York: Basic Books.

Gilligan, Carol. 1982. *In a different voice*. Cambridge: Harvard University Press.

Greene, Maxine. 1993. Diversity and inclusion: Toward a curriculum for human beings. *Teachers College Record* 95 (2): 211–221.

Hampshire, Stuart. 1989. *Innocence and experience*. Cambridge: Harvard University Press.

Haraway, Donna. 1989. *Primate visions: Gender, race, and nature in the world of modern science*. New York: Routledge.

Harding, Sandra. 1986. *The science question in feminism*. Ithaca, N.Y.: Cornell University Press.

Hubbard, Ruth. 1990. *The politics of women's biology*. New Brunswick: Rutgers University Press.

Hu-DeHart, Evelyn. 1993. Rethinking America: The practice and politics of multiculturalism in higher education. In *Beyond a dream deferred: Multicultural education and the politics of excellence*. Edited by Becky Thompson and Sangeeta Tyagi. Minneapolis: University of Minnesota Press.

Kant, Immanuel. 1987. *The critique of judgment*. Translated by Werner S. Pluhar. Indianapolis: Hackett Publishing.

Keller, Evelyn Fox. 1985. *Reflections on gender and science*. New Haven: Yale University Press.

Kettering Foundation. 1994. *Civic declaration: A call for a new citizenship*. Dayton, Ohio: American Civic Forum, The Kettering Foundation.

Kuhn, Thomas. 1970. *The structure of scientific revolutions*. 2d ed. Chicago: University of Chicago Press.

Madison, James. 1982. Federalist 10. In *The Federalist Papers*. Edited by Gary Wills. New York: Bantam Books.

Merleau-Ponty, Maurice. 1964. *Signs*. Translated by Richard C. McCleary. Evanston, Ill.: Northwestern University Press.

Miller, Jim. 1993. *The passion of Michel Foucault*. New York: Simon and Schuster.

Monk, Ray. 1990. *The duty of genius*. New York: Free Press/Maxwell-Macmillan.

Morrison, Toni. 1992. *Playing in the dark: Whiteness and the literary imagination*. Cambridge: Harvard University Press.

Newman, John Henry. 1982. *The idea of a university*. Edited by Martin J. Svaglic. Notre Dame: University of Notre Dame Press.

Nodding, Nell. 1984. *Caring*. Berkeley: University of California Press.

Pelikan, Jaroslav. 1992. *The idea of a university: A reexamination*. New Haven: Yale University Press.

Rich, Adrienne. 1993. *What is found there: Notebooks in poetry and politics*. New York: W.W. Norton.

Rosser, Sue V. 1994. *Biology and feminism: A dynamic interaction*. New York: Twayne-Macmillan.

Ruddick, Sara. 1989. *Maternal thinking*. Boston: Beacon Press.

Rudolph, Frederick. 1977. *Curriculum: A history of the American undergraduate course of study since 1636*. San Francisco: Jossey-Bass Publishers.

Takaki, Ronald. 1993. *A different mirror: A history of multicultural America*. Boston: Little, Brown.

Tocqueville, Alexis de. 1990. Reprint. Democracy in America. In *The American reader: Words that moved a nation*. Edited by Diane Ravitch. New York: Harper Collins. Original edition, London: Saunders and Otley, 1835.

West, Cornel. 1993. *Race matters*. Boston: Beacon Press.

Young, Iris Marion. 1990. *Justice and the politics of difference*. Princeton: Princeton University Press.

Young-Bruehl, Elisabeth. 1982. *Hannah Arendt: For love of the world*. New Haven: Yale University Press.

The data in the foreword on the racial recomposition in United States urban areas was compiled by Troy Duster, professor of sociology, University of California–Berkeley.